THE CREATIVITY OF DIMINISHMENT

SISTER ANKE

SLG PRESS
Convent of the Incarnation
Fairacres Oxford

ISBN 0 7283 0125 3
ISSN 0307-1405

This article first appeared in the 'Fairacres Chronicle', Winter 1987
First published in Fairacres Publications in 1990

Also published with 'Living with Retirement' by Oliver Tomkins
in *Into Another Intensity*, 1993.
Reprinted 1998

ACKNOWLEDGEMENT

We are grateful to the Sisters of Ordo Pacis for permission to publish this article

Printed by Will Print, Oxford

AS YOU CAN see from the title, there is a wonderful paradox in our subject: 'the creativity of diminishment'. I love this paradox and would like to unfold it a little bit, but I can only try to open some doors, to get some hints and glimpses very subjectively. It is a theme for all of us, and the Holy Spirit alone can lead us into its centre. His ways may be very different for each of us, to bring us thither, but there may be also a common stretch for us all.

Creativity is something very highly esteemed today. And I suppose we all have a little ideal of being a 'creative person' on some level or another. On the other side, diminishment is always something unwelcome. No one of us like to become less than we have been before—that goes dead against our feelings that we must grow, must become better, more, greater (let alone the fact that our economics always should grow; if they cease to grow, catastrophe seems already to have reached us!). And yet we cannot prevent them, diminishments are coming in our life on many levels. The typical process of diminishment, I think, is becoming less, not only for some time, but remaining less. And mostly the next step is becoming more less. To be diminished has obviously a downward trend, it is very near to the feeling of descending, going down the mountain. Creativity may have just the opposite direction: it brings us upwards, there is growing, new life, new hope.

So to speak of 'the creativity of diminishment' really is a paradox: creativity, growing upwards; diminishment, going downwards. And yet that is the truth. You know, surely, people who are in very bad situations and just that gives them strength to create something very good. For example, I think of a woman in Hamburg who was very ill with cancer, and she founded with her last strength an association for people who have cancer and created for them many possibilities to share their feelings and anxieties and to help each other. Really a marvellous creativity from a horrible diminishment which ended with her death.

But I would like to go to a still deeper level with our theme. John the Baptist says something amazing: 'He must increase, but I must decrease' (John 3:30 RSV). The Greek text in a literal translation is a very direct statement on our theme: 'Christ must grow, but I must be diminished!' in Greek, the passive voice! The paradox is revealed here as a change of dominion: no longer I but He! It is Christ in us, Christ in our world, who must grow, become more and more, He, the Creator, the Lord—and therefore we have to resign, to be diminished in a very real sense. Christ needs our whole being for this growing in us. 'It is no longer I who live, but Christ who lives in me' (Gal. 2:20). Christ now is the active one in growing Himself and in diminishing us. Our part is to let it happen to us, really to become less.

Therefore I would prefer a little modification of our theme to make it very clear: *God's* creativity in our diminishment. Christ said to Paul, 'My power is made perfect in weakness; (2 Cor. 12:9). Luther translated not quite so correctly but very personally, 'My power is made perfect in weak people'. Just in this sense I would like to explore our theme: God's creative power in our weakness, in our being diminished, in us the weak people we are. The paradox then highlights this further truth: God prefers the weakness, He loves the can't-ness—He who is the powerful one, to whom all things are possible. So Christ stands in the midst of our theme. His Cross is the very sign of the Father's mysterious creativity in the total diminishment of the Son. And here the paradox discloses its ultimate depth: God's creativity in God's diminishment, God's Resurrection in God's Death. And all our little experiences of being diminished (and of creativity too) will point to this mystery, far beyond our grasp.

In the end it is so simple. I was very impressed by a comment of Archbishop Anthony Bloom: he said, 'I am able to take my watch in my hand, my fingers hold it fast—but now my hand is occupied, it is no longer free for any other gift.' Being diminished by God means very often letting go of whatever we are holding to become open-handed for His grace. This letting go we experience mostly in a passive way at first, feeling it as being 'robbed', as a big loss; later on perhaps we are able to surrender the 'robbed thing', to give it to God freewillingly, and we can realise that then, paradoxically, the loss becomes a gain. Being robbed, letting go—diminishment in its full spiritual sense always is passive and active simultaneously.

God does not diminish us as a punishment or as an 'education' or because He is full of anger towards us sinners. If he diminishes us, it is to let us come nearer to Him, to make us more open for His grace to work in us. It is his creativity which does something very good in us, although our part in that game is to become less. But always the balance remains: He must grow and we must be diminished—half of this equation never comes into operation alone, always both parts together because God has bound them together in interdependence.

The inner attitude that reflects our willingness for God's diminishing us is the attitude of the open hands. Now one Latin word for 'to thank' is *gratiam referre*, that is, to bring back the grace to God. 'Return to Sender!'. Thanksgiving means therefore being ready to bring all we have received back in our open hands to God, praising and glorifying Him.

One could use the picture of a ball game for this truth: the father throws the ball to the child, the child throws it back then receives it anew—play of trustfully open hands, readiness to give, the to and fro of living love, which will remain even when the ball does not come back—the father is indeed more than the ball! Thanksgiving, bringing back the grace to God full of joyful trust, that is a door which leads directly into our theme: with such thanksgiving we 'allow' God to diminish us, to take back His gift, to work in us in a new way.

Our experiences of being diminished in this way are of course manifold. I would like to say a little bit about two experiences in our spiritual life we will all have to suffer over and over again. The first one seems to me to be that God tries (so often we resist!) to take away our ideals, first of all our pious ideals, to be or to become a good Christian, to pray very well and also to be very good in being diminished, in becoming old and so on. But we have to live in God's reality, and that means that we are not very ideal. For him that does not matter at all. We have to become as little and of no account as we really are, and in that state let God love us. Perhaps it belongs to a child to have fantasies of being omnipotent, as the psychologists say, but the older we become the more God wants us to live in his reality which is ours too, and not under the cloak of our wishes and fantasies.

The other diminishment I will describe will be for us all a painful one, I mean God's diminishments in our prayer life. How marvellous the beginning was! We really were able to pray, we loved to do it. And after some years? There this descent has already begun, we become less and less capable of praying. And after many years ? The downward mountain experiences are perhaps becoming unbearable: nothing of prayer seems to have remained, no ability at all for what we more and more long for. I fear such is the pattern, at least very often. It seems to be the usual way in a life of contemplative prayer. In the beginning perhaps we hoped it would go upwards more and more, but just the opposite does happen. We all know this growing can'tness in prayer, and we mostly do not see or feel that Christ is growing in us by that. He has not promised that we could grasp or even notice His growing in us, His creativity (which other people perhaps *can* see), whereas the loss of His gifts usually is a very hurtful feeling. Being diminished in this way brings us into the darkness, makes us blind and confused. It will help us to deep faith without seeing and 'having' something in our hands. Christ will grow in us totally unseen and in a way of which we cannot be conscious. That need not be a great mystical experience—but each of us will know it in a very deep and simple way. For example: one is in very exhausting professional work and the opportunities for 'proper prayer' are very small, then finally the holidays are coming, or we get sick and suddenly have lots of time; but prayer is worse than before. Or perhaps we are at last in retirement, now therefore we have time and space and 'plans' for a 'real' spiritual life. But our prayer-life does not blossom, it seems to fade away. Of course we have to 'do' whatever we can in spite of our can't-ness, but the experience of a descent will more and more be there. And we have perhaps bitterly to learn that there will never be an ideal state in our life. As I said earlier, we are not ideals we have to realize the reality. But Christ is—unseen—in the midst of our so very evident nothingness, and He loves us just as we are.

As younger ones we have more chances to run away from the diminishments on so many levels—life is so open and presents so many opportunities and compensations. Becoming older means the circle is becoming narrower, the ways out are more and more blocked, we have to stand, whether we want to or not. The same experience we have to meet in serious illness, whether we are young or old, also in bereavement. In any case, then the reality of the 'descending life' becomes unavoidable. So I would like to say something about the diminishments of coming to that phase in our life which is called 'menopause'; about the letting go of our professional work when we come to retirement, the letting go of dear people through their death (more often demanded of us the older we become); and about dying.

First I will tell you a very personal experience, which seems to be so helpful for our letting go totally, for this 'creative No' to which Wendy Robinson has already called our attention (in her essay, 'Sounding Stones'). My father died last year and he had a very long and hard agony of two days. I had a very good and deep relationship with him and he with me, so I was really very near to him in these hours which he had to struggle through when he was relatively quite conscious. At last, of course, I was very tired, and nobody knew how long it would go on. So they said to me I should sleep a little bit. I did and it was a real letting go of him. And after half an hour he could die (I was called and was again with him). I am deeply convinced that my letting him be alone with the others, this letting him go, is connected with *his* being able to let go, to die. Surely an irrational thing. But I would like to give it to you as an example of this No which sets free creativity in a very mysterious way. Our obedient No, our going away, our letting go, can really help others—much more perhaps than our Yes of helpfulness, our being with them, our caring for them. Perhaps for all of us again and again this point of letting go will come and will help others; to die or, of course, really to live, to grow, to become mature.

In this connection I am thinking of retirement. It is always a being diminished. And many people today experience their retirement as a very hard thing because becoming older and being without 'achievement' in work is seen as a big loss. We cannot escape from this current climate of thought. Of course we know that our worth is given us by God and one need not be disturbed by contemporary ideas, but we have to endure exposure to such assumptions and to learn in them the real truth: God's creativity in our diminishment. We have to learn to say our No: to our work, to colleagues, to friends, to the family, to our Sisters, we have to leave our 'throne' (if we sat on one!). And we shall experience that God can do marvellous things for others if we have said our 'creative No' to them with love and with our whole heart, because God wants that from us now. If we are 'irreplaceable' we hinder God at the end from doing His works. The more we learn to say this wholehearted No, the more we shall discover lots of God's creativity in situations which seem to be nothing else than 'impossible'.

Now something else in this phase of our life which is so often a difficulty for us is the menopause. It belongs very much to our theme because it is really a diminishment. However our life may have been till that phase and however we have dealt with our sexuality, as women we go through a real bereavement in these years. We are really bereaved of our fruitfulness and that means, so I think, we have lost a great value in our being women. It is something of a major diminishment. And therefore these years are years of crisis. If you read helpful books about the menopause they will teach you how rich you remain in spite of the loss, and how life can be wonderful in spite of this experience. That is true. But it seems to me that the other side of this phase is the more important one: to pass through real dying as a pre-exercise for the later dying of the whole being. What a challenge to let God work and be creative in us in His way by this being diminished, by this becoming older, by this dying! Wendy Robinson perhaps would speak of the challenge of our creative No to our fruitfulness, to our life as women till now (whether married or lived in celibacy) and it will go on in another way. We'll become more mature, we 'know' more of death, we are more ready to be prepared for it by God and in His ways in our whole being.

A little appendix to a special diminishment of this phase: we have to observe a very important change in the 'hierarchy' of our being. Till now usually our mind or our will could command our body what to do, what not to do. The menopause begins in the body as a part of dying, and from then on it, our body, begins more and more to take command, whether we like it or not. For many of us that too is a diminishment: to be forced to have regard to our body, to be obedient to it. But I think that is a great opportunity for God to help us to become 'one' in ourselves, to learn to be reconciled with this body, which will become older and older and more frail and in the end will give the sign for death. I like to see how true and reliable our body is, it works and helps us to live, even when we are very bad to it, do not like it, are 'against it' in a probably misunderstood 'asceticism'. The body is always our fellow and ally, we have to make our pilgrimage with it in unity. Fasting, for example, is for me something to be done with my body as an ally and not against it, because the whole being is to be turned to God. The phase of the menopause, this letting go, can teach us a very new relation to our body—a deep help from God for the coming years till the end of our life. I was very moved by a letter written by an old deaconess in Germany at the beginning of this century. Late in her nineties she wrote a letter full of thankfulness for her body and she counted up her senses and limbs and thanked each for its true service and allowed them now to be lazy, to go off duty; she allowed herself to be deaf and blind and lame. That is for me a deep work of God's creativity in a very diminished old woman. God had made her really one in herself—helpful for lots of people!

One step further. Perhaps you know the expression which is very important for the brothers of Taizé: 'The resurrected Christ celebrates His feast of reconciliation in us without ending'. I like to imagine this phrase, to 'see' the feast of Christ in me. There is a wonderful banquet-hall, full of light and joy, a large table, Christ as the Master of the Feast sitting as president at this table. And round the table 'I' am sitting, my whole being with all its parts, which constitute my human existence, some known, some half-known, most perhaps unconscious. They are all invited to come to Christ's feast in me, no one is excluded or expelled. Christ invites them all. I am very often rather horrified that all are allowed to come. And I have to greet them, to lead them to the table and so on. A picture for our being reconciled as a person in Christ! It is a very good exercise to let your 'people' come to this feast of Christ: for example, let your body come, let your fear come, your guilty feeling, your memories, you super-ego.

One day my old age came into the hall. That is a very funny story (and you see, I am not *very* old at present) . This old age was a small, very ancient and joyful person. She told me how she works. She said to me: I'll take away from you one thing after another, perhaps beginning with your teeth, your hair, looking young and fresh and so on. You have the choice. If you give me freewillingly what I want to have, I will bring it and give it to Christ as your gift; if you refuse, I will rob you of it, because I am much stronger than you, and put it in my own pocket! I was very amazed by this lesson, but I think it is a wonderful picture for our theme: Christ can be very creative in us when we are ready to be diminished, to let go our strength, our youth, all we are, in becoming older and older, His challenges for obedience will grow—and the challenges to new creation within us.

I have to stop, but I cannot help telling you one 'picture' more: a picture of my death which of course too is in the banquet hall of Christ within me. But this picture was also on a deeper level, somewhere in my unconscious, There was a circular lake, rather small, and very slowly my death ascended in the middle of that lake. It was the classical skeleton with a wide black cape, the hood drawn over his skull. Christ beckoned Death and slowly he went on the water till he reached the land and came into my consciousness. I had to meet him, to greet him, to give him the kiss of peace, because it was *my* death. And then both of us were blessed by Christ and sent into the river of baptism, to be baptised together into the death of Christ. So both of us went into the river hand in hand. There were steps in the river and very slowly we went down. Death was at my right hand. It was a very deep and silent experience. We were now totally under the water, but it was like a shelter round us, the shelter of Chris's death, a protecting darkness. And step by step we went down. Suddenly I noticed in the darkness that I had somebody at my left hand too, and then I noticed that it was a very long row of persons, which went with us step by step, very concentrated, silent, slow. And I realised that all my feast-fellows were with me going down the stairs.

For a long time I did not know who was going next to me and holding my left hand. But suddenly I knew; it was my body! And then I knew: It was a picture of our life in Christ and of our death in Christ. We go downstairs with our whole being step by step, and dying means to us that our body will suddenly let go our hand, and our death will embrace us and fall downwards with us. The whole festival party will fall downwards. But in the depths there is the Resurrection. The Resurrection is below! Our life will be for us probably more and more like a descent, a descent into becoming old and without any more 'achievement' and totally dependent on others. Yes, life is a descent, a going downwards, a real and irresistible being diminished, but the Resurrection is below We will be totally gathered into it. God's creation will be finished in the depth, in the abyss of Resurrection.